Delicious
bite-size

Delicious

bite-size

LOVE FOOD

Love Food ® is an imprint of Parragon Books Ltd

Parragon
Queen Street House
4 Queen Street
Bath BA1 1HE, UK

Introduction by Frances Eames
Photography by Günter Beer
Home Economist Stevan Paul

ISBN 978-1-4075-1624-0

Printed in China

Notes for reader
• This book uses metric and imperial measurements. Follow the same units of measurement throughout; do not mix imperial and metric.
• All spoon measurements are level: teaspoons are assumed to be 5 ml and tablespoons are assumed to be 15 ml.
• Unless otherwise stated, milk is assumed to be semi-skimmed and eggs are medium. The times given are an approximate guide only.
• Some recipes contain nuts. If you are allergic to nuts you should avoid using them and any products containing nuts.
• Recipes using raw or very lightly cooked eggs should be avoided by infants, the elderly, pregnant women, convalescents and anyone suffering from illness.
• Vegans should be aware that some of the ready-made ingredients in the recipes in this book may be derived from animal products.
• Vegetarians should be aware that some of the ready-made ingredients in the recipes in this book may contain meat or meat products.

Contents

Bite-size

A morsel of something delicious and tantalizing is all you need to make the perfect party. Bite-size entertaining is well and truly back in vogue. For gourmet menus with the minimum of effort, try the fabulous collection of recipe ideas inside this book.

Bite-size dining is great for any occasion and can be as chic or as informal as you want. Forget stuffy seating plans and masses of silver cutlery – this season it's all about getting fun and friendly. You could host an early evening cocktail party accompanied by a light and delicious buffet, or turn a drinks party into a real occasion with a really sumptuous spread.

Don't be daunted by making your own canapés. They are easy to prepare in advance, look fantastic and are sure to create a good impression. For maximum impact nibbles should emphasize visual style as well as taste; colour, shape and texture are all important. From traditional and much-loved classics to more modern and exotic creations, this book provides a palette of flavours from across the globe.

Choosing the menu

Setting the menu is crucial in determining the mood and feel of your gathering. Think about the evening's occasion, the season and the guests' requirements. For a luxurious cocktail party, pick the most impressive-looking dishes. If you are hosting a small and intimate gathering then you may focus the menu on your friends' favourite foods. For a summer soirée, you may decide to plan vegetable and seafood dishes for *al fresco* eating. Think about what vegetables are in season and shop no earlier than the day before the party to ensure you get the freshest ingredients. Most importantly, your menu should contain a variety of

colours, textures and shapes. Don't forget to ask any vegetarian, gluten-free or dairy-free diners to give you prior warning of special requirements.

Preparation
Once you have chosen an array of delicacies you can plan your strategy. Make a list of ingredients and shop the day before. It is important to prepare what you can in advance and refrigerate. This will leave you with time to organize the house and plan your outfit with plenty of time to spare. Make sure you work in an organized space; clean down work surfaces between each dish and wash up as you go to maintain a calm and serene kitchen. You can always ask friends to prepare a specific bite and give them the recipe in advance.

Presentation
Presentation is the key to producing a breathtaking

spread. Serving platters and bowls should be attractive, spotless and matching. You may want to theme the crockery; for example, try chic Japanese platters or colourful Mediterranean dishes. You could include different-shaped plates and bowls, or serve food on wooden boards. All white or all black dishes can be quite striking, and they provide a simple canvas for the attractive nibbles.

If you aren't able to match the crockery then try lining dishes with simple but effective napkins; that way a theme is maintained without a matching set. Keep garnishes to a minimum so as not to distract from the food. Small, practical details can make the difference between a messy eating experience and a sophisticated party. Provide small glasses for used skewers, several finger bowls with lemons and plenty of attractive napkins.

Canapés

makes 20

plain flour, for dusting

200 g/7 oz ready-made puff
pastry, thawed if frozen

3 tbsp pesto

20 cherry tomatoes, each cut
into 3 slices

115 g/4 oz goat's cheese

salt and pepper

fresh basil sprigs, to garnish

pesto & goat's cheese tartlets

Preheat the oven to 200°C/400°F/Gas Mark 6, then lightly flour a baking sheet. Roll out the pastry on a floured work surface to 3 mm/⅛ inch thick. Cut out 20 rounds with a 5-cm/2-inch plain cutter and arrange the pastry rounds on the floured baking sheet.

Spread a little pesto on each round, leaving a margin around the edge, then arrange 3 tomato slices on top of each one.

Crumble the goat's cheese over and season to taste with salt and pepper. Bake in the preheated oven for 10 minutes, or until the pastry is puffed up, crisp and golden. Garnish with basil sprigs and serve warm.

spanish spinach & tomato pizzas

makes 32

2 tbsp extra virgin olive oil, plus extra for brushing and drizzling

1 onion, finely chopped

1 garlic clove, finely chopped

400 g/14 oz canned chopped tomatoes

125 g/4¹/2 oz baby spinach leaves

25 g/1 oz pine nuts

salt and pepper

for the bread dough

100 ml/3¹/2 fl oz warm water

¹/2 tsp easy-blend dried yeast

pinch of sugar

200 g/7 oz strong white flour, plus extra for dusting

¹/2 tsp salt

To make the bread dough, measure the water into a small bowl, sprinkle in the dried yeast and sugar and leave in a warm place for 10–15 minutes, or until frothy.

Meanwhile, sift the flour and salt into a large bowl. Make a well in the centre of the flour and pour in the yeast liquid, then mix together with a wooden spoon. Using your hands, work the mixture until it leaves the sides of the bowl clean.

Turn the dough out on to a lightly floured work surface and knead for 10 minutes, or until smooth and elastic and no longer sticky. Shape into a ball and put it in a clean bowl. Cover with a clean, damp tea towel and leave in a warm place for 1 hour, or until it has risen and doubled in size.

To make the topping, heat the oil in a large, heavy-based frying pan. Add the onion and cook for 5 minutes, or until soft. Add the garlic and cook for 30 seconds. Stir in the tomatoes and cook for 5 minutes, stirring occasionally, until reduced to a thick mixture. Add the spinach leaves and cook, stirring, until wilted. Season to taste with salt and pepper.

While the dough is rising, preheat the oven to 200°C/400°F/Gas Mark 6. Brush several baking trays with olive oil. Turn the dough out on to a lightly floured work surface and knead well for 2–3 minutes to knock out the air bubbles. Roll out the dough very thinly and, using a 6-cm/2½-inch plain, round cutter, cut out 32 rounds. Place on the prepared baking sheets.

Spread each base with the spinach mixture, sprinkle over the pine nuts and drizzle with a little of the olive oil. Bake in the oven for 10–15 minutes, or until the edges are golden.

makes 8

1 small French baguette

4 tomatoes, thinly sliced

4 hard-boiled eggs

4 bottled or canned anchovy
fillets in olive oil, drained
and halved lengthways

8 marinated stoned black
olives

for the tapenade

100 g/3 1/2 oz stoned black
olives

6 bottled or canned anchovy
fillets in olive oil, drained

2 tbsp capers, rinsed

2 garlic cloves, roughly
chopped

1 tsp Dijon mustard

2 tbsp lemon juice

1 tsp fresh thyme leaves

4–5 tbsp olive oil

pepper

egg & tapenade toasts

To make the tapenade, place the olives, anchovies, capers, garlic, mustard, lemon juice, thyme and pepper to taste in a food processor and process for 20–25 seconds, or until smooth. Scrape down the sides of the mixing bowl. With the motor running, gradually add the oil through the feeder tube to make a smooth paste. Spoon the paste into a bowl, cover with clingfilm and set aside until required.

Preheat the grill to medium. Cut the French baguette into 8 slices, discarding the crusty ends. Toast on both sides under the hot grill until light golden brown. Leave to cool.

To assemble the toasts, spread a little of the tapenade on 1 side of each slice of toast. Top with the tomato slices. Shell the hard-boiled eggs, then slice and arrange over the tomatoes. Dot each egg slice with a little of the remaining tapenade and top with anchovies. Halve the marinated olives and arrange 2 halves on each toast. Serve immediately.

makes 24

4 spring onions, white parts and half the green parts, very finely chopped

1/2 lemon, sliced

1 bay leaf, torn in half

1/2 tsp black peppercorns, lightly crushed

125 ml/4 fl oz dry white wine

450 g/1 lb boneless salmon, cut into pieces

115 g/4 oz butter, at room temperature

140 g/5 oz smoked salmon, cut into pieces

1/4 tsp ground nutmeg

2 tbsp very finely chopped fresh parsley

salt and pepper

12 large slices country-style bread, such as sourdough, each about 1 cm/1/2 inch thick

smoked salmon pâté

Put the onions, lemon slices, bay leaf, peppercorns and white wine in a large frying pan, add water to half-fill the pan and bring to the boil. Boil for 2 minutes, and then reduce the heat to its lowest setting. Add the salmon pieces, cover the pan and leave to simmer for 8 minutes. Remove the pan from the heat, keep covered and allow the salmon to cool in the cooking liquid.

Meanwhile, melt 25 g/1 oz of the butter in a large frying pan over a medium heat. Add the smoked salmon pieces and nutmeg and stir for about 2 minutes, until the salmon loses its shiny coral colour and becomes opaque. Remove from the heat and set aside until cool.

Drain and flake the poached salmon and put into a wide, shallow bowl. Add the smoked salmon mixture and cooking juices, the remaining butter and use your fingers to mix it all together until the salmon is very finely mixed. Stir in the parsley. Taste and adjust the seasoning, although you probably won't need much salt because of the flavour of the smoked salmon. Spoon into a bowl, cover and chill until 30 minutes before you are ready to serve.

When you are ready to serve, preheat the grill to high. Toast the bread on both sides until golden brown and crisp, then cut each slice in half. Spread the salmon pâté on the hot toast and serve.

serves 4

2 tbsp butter, melted, plus extra for greasing

225 g/8 oz waxy potatoes, finely diced

500 g/1 lb 2 oz fresh baby spinach

2 tbsp water

1 tomato, deseeded and chopped

1/4 tsp chilli powder

1/2 tsp lemon juice

225 g/8 oz (8 sheets) filo pastry, thawed if frozen

salt and pepper

potato & spinach triangles

Preheat the oven to 190°C/375°F/Gas Mark 5. Lightly grease a baking tray with a little butter. Cook the potatoes in a saucepan of lightly salted boiling water for 10 minutes, or until tender. Drain thoroughly and place in a mixing bowl.

Meanwhile, put the spinach into a large saucepan with the water, cover and cook, stirring occasionally, over a low heat for 2 minutes, or until wilted. Drain the spinach thoroughly, squeezing out the excess moisture, and add to the potatoes. Stir in the tomato, chilli powder and lemon juice. Season to taste with salt and pepper.

Lightly brush the sheets of filo pastry with melted butter. Spread out 4 of the sheets and lay a second sheet on top of each. Cut them into rectangles about 20 x 10 cm/8 x 4 inches.

Spoon a portion of the potato and spinach mixture onto one end of each rectangle. Fold a corner of the pastry over the filling, fold the pointed end back over the pastry strip, then fold over the remaining pastry to form a triangle.

Place the triangles on the prepared baking tray and bake in the preheated oven for 20 minutes, or until golden brown. Serve hot or cold.

makes 20

1 thin French baguette,
cut into 20 slices

*for the gorgonzola &
caramelized onion topping*

2 large onions, thinly sliced

25 g/1 oz butter

40 g/1½ oz caster sugar

225 ml/8 fl oz water

175 g/6 oz gorgonzola cheese

*for the tomato, avocado &
bacon topping*

55 g/2 oz chopped bacon

1 tbsp olive oil

1 large tomato, cored,
deseeded and finely diced

1–2 tbsp lemon juice

1–2 tbsp extra virgin olive oil

2 tbsp finely shredded basil
leaves

pinch of sugar

1 avocado

salt and pepper

topped crostini

Preheat the grill and place the bread slices on the grill rack about 10 cm/4 inches from the source of the heat. Toast slowly for 6–8 minutes, turning once, until crisp and golden on both sides. Leave to cool.

To make the caramelized onions, put the onions, butter and half the sugar in a saucepan with the water and bring to the boil. Reduce the heat and simmer, uncovered, for about 20 minutes until the onions are tender and the water has evaporated. Transfer the onions to a frying pan, sprinkle with the remaining sugar and stir over medium-high heat until the sugar melts and the onions are a light golden brown.

To make the tomato, avocado and bacon topping, put the chopped bacon and olive oil in a frying pan over medium-high heat and stir for about 5 minutes until the bacon is crisp. Remove from the pan, drain on kitchen paper and then transfer to a bowl. Add the tomato dice, lemon juice, olive oil, basil, sugar and salt and pepper to taste and stir. Cut the avocado in half, remove the stone and peel, then finely dice the flesh. Add to the bowl and gently stir together, making sure the avocado is well coated so it doesn't turn brown; add extra lemon juice or olive oil, if necessary.

When ready to serve, cover 10 crostini with a small slice of gorgonzola cheese, then top with a dollop of the caramelized onions. Top the remaining crostini with the tomato, avocado and bacon mixture. Arrange the crostini on large platters and serve.

makes 30

3 large potatoes, cut into chunks

85 g/3 oz frozen peas

55 g/2 oz frozen sweetcorn kernels, thawed

2 shallots, finely chopped

1 tsp ground cumin

1 tsp ground coriander

2 fresh green chillies, deseeded and finely chopped

2 tbsp chopped fresh mint

2 tbsp chopped fresh coriander

4 tbsp lemon juice

15 sheets filo pastry (about 12 x 18 cm/4^{1}/$_{2}$ x 7 inches), thawed if frozen

melted butter, for brushing

groundnut or sunflower oil, for deep-frying

mango chutney, to serve

salt

vegetable samosas

Place the potatoes in a saucepan and add cold water to cover and a pinch of salt. Bring to the boil, then reduce the heat, cover and simmer for 15–20 minutes, or until tender. Meanwhile, cook the peas according to the instructions on the packet, then drain. Drain the potatoes, return to the saucepan and mash coarsely with a potato masher or fork. Add the peas to the potatoes, then transfer to a bowl.

Add the sweetcorn, shallots, cumin, ground coriander, chillies, mint, fresh coriander and lemon juice and season to taste with salt. Mix well.

Keep the filo pastry sheets covered with clingfilm to prevent them from drying out. Take a sheet of filo, brush with melted butter and cut in half lengthways. Place a tablespoonful of the filling in a corner of the pastry strip. Fold the pastry over at right angles to make a triangle, enclosing the filling. Continue folding in this way all the way down the strip to make a triangular parcel. Repeat with the remaining pastry sheets and filling.

Heat the oil in a deep-fat fryer or large saucepan to 180–190°C/350–375°F, or until a cube of bread browns in 30 seconds. Add the samosas, in batches, and cook until golden brown. Remove with a slotted spoon and drain on kitchen paper. Alternatively, bake the samosas in a preheated oven at 200°C/400°F/Gas Mark 6, for 10–15 minutes, or until golden brown. Serve the samosas hot or at room temperature with mango chutney.

makes 72

4 skinless, boneless chicken thighs

100 g/3¹/2 oz cooked, peeled prawns

1 small egg, beaten

3 spring onions, finely chopped

2 garlic cloves, crushed

2 tbsp chopped fresh coriander

1 tbsp fish sauce

12 slices white bread, crusts removed

75 g/2³/4 oz sesame seeds

sunflower oil, for frying

salt and pepper

shredded spring onion curls, to garnish

prawn & chicken sesame toasts

Place the chicken and prawns in a food processor and process until very finely chopped. Add the egg, spring onions, garlic, coriander, fish sauce and pepper and salt to taste and pulse for a few seconds to mix well. Transfer to a large bowl.

Spread the mixture evenly over the slices of bread, right to the edges. Sprinkle the sesame seeds over a plate and press the chicken-and-prawn-topped side of each slice of bread into them to coat evenly.

Using a sharp knife, cut the bread into small squares, making 6 per slice.

Heat a 1-cm/¹/2-inch depth of oil in a wide frying pan until very hot. Shallow-fry the bread rectangles quickly, in batches, for 2–3 minutes, or until golden brown all over, turning them over once.

Drain the toasts well on kitchen paper, transfer to a serving dish and garnish with shredded spring onion curls. Serve hot.

makes 12

100 g/4 oz puff pastry rolled
to a depth of 3mm/¹/₈ inch

4 large fresh scallops,
cleaned and roe removed

salt and pepper

extra virgin olive oil for
coating the scallops

for the pea & mint purée

50 g/2 oz cooked peas

small clove garlic, grated

1 tbsp extra virgin olive oil

1 tbsp chopped mint

1 tbsp soured cream

1 tsp lemon juice

salt and pepper

mini tartlets with scallops & pea & mint purée

Preheat the oven to 180°C/ 350°F/Gas Mark 4. Using a 4-cm/
1¹/₂-inch round pastry cutter, cut out 12 pastry discs. Re-roll
and use the puff pastry leftovers if there is not enough to
make 12 discs.

Place the pastry discs on a flat tray, lined with greaseproof paper.
Lay another layer of greaseproof paper over the top and then
place a slightly smaller flat tray on top. (This will prevent the
puff pastry from rising in the oven.)

Leave the pastry to rest for 20 minutes in a cool place before
baking in the oven for 15–20 minutes or until golden. Remove
and leave to cool.

To make the pea and mint purée, blend the peas in a food
processor and add the garlic, extra virgin olive oil, mint, soured
cream, lemon juice, salt and pepper. Process until combined.
Scrape the mixture into a small container and place in the
refrigerator.

Heat a non-stick frying pan until just smoking. Toss the scallops
in a little extra virgin olive oil and season with salt and pepper.
Add the scallops to the pan and cook for 30 seconds each side.
Remove the scallops from the pan and set aside.

To assemble the canapés, place a small amount of pea and mint
purée on each mini tartlet. Cut each scallop into 3 slices and
arrange on top of the canapés. Serve immediately.

serves 4

125 ml/4 fl oz extra virgin
olive oil

8 x 1-cm/^{1}/$_2$-inch thick slices
baguette or ciabatta

115 g/4 oz goat's cheese

1 tbsp finely snipped fresh
chives

pepper

goat's cheese & chive croûtons

Preheat the oven to 180°C/350°F/Gas Mark 4. Pour the oil into a shallow dish and place the bread in the dish. Leave for 1–2 minutes, then turn and leave for a further 2 minutes. The bread should be thoroughly saturated in oil.

Meanwhile, if the cheese has come in a log, cut into 8 slices. If the cheese has come in rounds, crumble coarsely.

Place the bread on a baking tray and bake in the preheated oven for 5 minutes. Remove the tray from the oven, turn the bread over and top each slice with cheese. Sprinkle generously with pepper.

Return the tray to the oven for a further 5 minutes to heat the cheese thoroughly. Remove from the oven, arrange the croûtons on plates and sprinkle with chives. Serve immediately.

Elegant Nibbles

serves 6–8

4 large skinless, boneless chicken breasts

5 tbsp extra virgin olive oil

1 onion, finely chopped

6 garlic cloves, finely chopped

grated rind of 1 lemon, finely pared rind of 1 lemon and juice of both lemons

4 tbsp chopped fresh flat-leaf parsley

salt and pepper

lemon wedges and crusty bread, to serve

chicken in lemon & garlic

Using a sharp knife, slice the chicken breasts widthways into very thin slices. Heat the olive oil in a large, heavy-based frying pan, add the onion and fry for 5 minutes, or until softened but not browned. Add the garlic and fry for a further 30 seconds.

Add the sliced chicken to the pan and fry gently for 5–10 minutes, stirring from time to time, until all the ingredients are lightly browned and the chicken is tender.

Add the grated lemon rind and the lemon juice and let it bubble. At the same time, deglaze the pan by scraping and stirring all the bits on the base of the pan into the juices with a wooden spoon. Remove the pan from the heat, stir in the parsley and season to taste with salt and pepper.

Transfer the chicken in lemon and garlic, piping hot, to a warmed serving dish. Sprinkle with the pared lemon rind, and serve with lemon wedges for squeezing over the chicken, accompanied by chunks or slices of crusty bread for mopping up the lemon and garlic juices.

makes 12

350 g/12 oz monkfish tail or
250 g/9 oz monkfish fillet

12 stalks of fresh rosemary

3 tbsp extra virgin olive oil

juice of 1/2 small lemon

1 garlic clove, crushed

salt and pepper

6 thick back bacon rashers

aïoli (see page 87), to serve

monkfish, rosemary & bacon skewers

If using monkfish tail, cut either side of the central bone with a sharp knife and remove the flesh to form 2 fillets. Slice the fillets in half lengthways, then cut each fillet into 12 bite-size chunks to give a total of 24 pieces. Put the monkfish pieces in a large bowl.

To prepare the rosemary skewers, strip the leaves off the stalks and reserve them, leaving a few leaves at one end.

For the marinade, finely chop the reserved leaves and whisk together in a bowl with the olive oil, lemon juice, garlic and salt and pepper to taste. Add the monkfish pieces and toss until coated in the marinade. Cover and leave to marinate in the refrigerator for 1–2 hours.

Preheat the grill to medium-high and arrange the skewers on the grill pan so that the leaves of the rosemary skewers protrude from the grill and therefore do not catch fire during cooking. Grill the monkfish and bacon skewers for 10 minutes, turning from time to time and basting with any remaining marinade, or until cooked. Serve hot accompanied by a bowl of aïoli in which to dip them.

makes 24

for the blinis

85 g/3 oz plain flour

1 tsp dried yeast

1/2 tsp sugar

150 ml/5 fl oz warm water

85 g/3 oz buckwheat flour

125 ml/4 fl oz warm milk

40 g/1 1/2 oz butter, melted and cooled

1 large egg, separated

vegetable oil, for cooking

salt and pepper

for the topping

85 g/3 oz soured cream

finely grated rind of 2 lemons

55 g/2 oz smoked salmon, very finely sliced

pepper

2 tbsp very finely snipped chives, to garnish

smoked salmon blinis

To make the blinis, stir the flour, yeast and sugar together in a bowl. Make a well in the centre and slowly add the water, drawing in flour from the side to make a wet, lumpy batter. Beat until the batter is smooth, then stir in the buckwheat flour, cover the bowl tightly with a tea towel and set aside for 1 hour, until the batter has risen and the surface is covered with air bubbles.

Meanwhile, mix the soured cream with the lemon rind and pepper to taste. Cover and chill until ready to use. Stir the milk, butter and egg yolk together with a generous pinch of salt and pepper, then add to the batter, stirring well until blended. Beat the egg white in a separate bowl until peaks form, and then fold into the batter.

Heat a large frying pan over medium heat until you can feel the heat rising, then lightly brush the surface all over with vegetable oil using crumpled kitchen paper. Fill a tablespoon measure two-thirds full with the batter, then drop the batter on to the hot surface so it forms a circle about 5 cm/2 inches across; add as many more as will fit in the pan without touching. Cook for just over a minute, or until the top surface is covered with air holes and the bottom is golden brown and set. Use a palette knife to flip over the blinis and cook until set and golden brown. Transfer to a heatproof plate and keep warm in a low oven while you cook the remaining batter.

To serve, arrange the warm, not hot, blinis on a platter and top each with about 2 teaspoons of the chilled soured cream. Lay the salmon strips over the soured cream, add the snipped chives and serve.

makes 24

3 medium-sized heads
chicory

115 g/4 oz blue cheese, such
as Stilton, finely crumbled

4 tbsp pecan halves,
very finely chopped

1 punnet mustard cress,
to garnish

for the dressing

100 ml/3^{1}/$_{2}$ fl oz extra virgin
olive oil

2^{1}/$_{2}$ tbsp balsamic vinegar

1 tsp Dijon mustard

1 tsp sugar

salt and pepper

pretty chicory bites

To make the dressing, put the oil, vinegar, mustard, sugar and salt and pepper to taste in a screw-top jar and shake until blended. Taste and adjust the seasoning, then set aside until required.

Cut the edges off the chicory heads so you can separate the leaves. Pick over the leaves and select the 24 best, boat-shaped leaves, then rinse them and pat dry.

Put the cheese and pecans in a bowl and gently toss together. Add 2 tablespoons of the dressing and toss again.

Arrange the chicory leaves on serving platters, then put a teaspoon of the cheese and pecans towards the pointed end of each leaf. Add small pieces of mustard cress to each to garnish. Cover and chill for up to an hour before serving.

serves 6

450 g/1 lb prepared squid

plain flour, for coating

sunflower oil, for deep-frying

salt

lemon wedges, to garnish

aïoli (see page 87), to serve

calamares

Slice the squid into 1-cm/½-inch rings and halve the tentacles if large. Rinse and dry well on kitchen paper so that they do not spit during cooking. Dust the squid rings with flour so that they are lightly coated.

Heat the sunflower oil in a deep fryer to 180–190°C/350–375°F, or until a cube of bread browns in 30 seconds. Carefully add the squid rings, in batches so that the temperature of the oil does not drop, and fry for 2–3 minutes, or until golden brown and crisp all over, turning several times. Do not overcook as the squid will become tough and rubbery rather than moist and tender.

Using a slotted spoon, remove the fried squid from the deep fryer and drain well on kitchen paper. Keep hot in a warm oven while you fry the remaining squid rings.

Sprinkle the fried squid rings with salt and serve piping hot, garnished with lemon wedges for squeezing over them. Accompany with a bowl of aïoli in which to dip the calamares.

serves 6–8

200 g/7 oz Manchego cheese

3 tbsp plain flour

1 egg

1 tsp water

85 g/3 oz fresh white or
brown breadcrumbs

sunflower oil, for deep-frying

salt and pepper

fried manchego cheese

Slice the cheese into triangular shapes about 2 cm/¾ inch thick or alternatively into cubes measuring about the same size. Put the flour in a polythene bag and season with salt and pepper to taste. Break the egg into a shallow dish and beat together with the water. Spread the breadcrumbs on to a plate.

Toss the cheese pieces in the flour so that they are evenly coated, then dip the cheese in the egg mixture. Finally, dip the cheese in the breadcrumbs so that the pieces are coated on all sides. Transfer to a large plate and store in the refrigerator until you are ready to serve them.

Just before serving, heat about 2.5 cm/1 inch of the sunflower oil in a large, heavy-based frying pan or heat the oil in a deep fryer to 180–190°C/350–375°F, or until a cube of bread browns in 30 seconds. Add the cheese pieces, in batches of about 4 or 5 pieces so that the temperature of the oil does not drop, and fry for 1–2 minutes, turning once, until the cheese is just beginning to melt and they are golden brown on all sides. Do make sure that the oil is hot enough otherwise the coating on the cheese will take too long to become crisp and the cheese inside may ooze out.

Using a slotted spoon, remove the fried cheese from the frying pan or deep fryer and drain well on kitchen paper. Serve the fried cheese pieces hot, accompanied by cocktail sticks on which to spear them.

serves 8

800 g/1 lb 12 oz fresh
mussels, in their shells

splash of dry white wine

1 bay leaf

85 g/3 oz butter

35 g/1¼ oz fresh white or
brown breadcrumbs

4 tbsp chopped fresh flat-leaf
parsley, plus extra sprigs to
garnish

2 tbsp snipped fresh chives

2 garlic cloves, finely chopped

salt and pepper

lemon wedges, to serve

mussels with herb & garlic butter

Clean the mussels by scrubbing or scraping the shells and pulling out any beards that are attached to them. Discard any with broken shells and any that refuse to close when tapped. Put the mussels in a colander and rinse well under cold running water. Preheat the oven to 230°C/450°F/Gas Mark 8.

Put the mussels in a large saucepan and add a splash of wine and the bay leaf. Cook, covered, over a high heat for 5 minutes, shaking the saucepan occasionally, or until the mussels are opened. Drain the mussels and discard any that remain closed.

Shell the mussels, reserving one half of each shell. Arrange the mussels, in their half shells, in a large, shallow, ovenproof serving dish.

Melt the butter and pour into a small bowl. Add the breadcrumbs, parsley, chives, garlic and salt and pepper to taste and mix well together. Leave until the butter has set slightly. Using your fingers or 2 teaspoons, take a large pinch of the herb and butter mixture and use to fill each mussel shell, pressing it down well. Chill the filled mussels in the refrigerator until ready to serve.

To serve, bake the mussels in the oven for 10 minutes, or until hot. Serve immediately, garnished with parsley sprigs and accompanied by lemon wedges for squeezing over them.

makes 12

450 g/1 lb lean boneless pork

3 tbsp extra virgin olive oil,
plus extra for oiling (optional)

grated rind and juice of
1 large lemon

2 garlic cloves, crushed

2 tbsp chopped fresh flat-leaf
parsley, plus extra to garnish

1 tbsp ras-el-hanout spice
blend

salt and pepper

miniature pork brochettes

The brochettes are marinated overnight, so remember to do this in advance in order that they are ready when you need them. Cut the pork into pieces about 2 cm/¾ inch square and put in a large, shallow, non-metallic dish that will hold the pieces in a single layer.

To prepare the marinade, put all the remaining ingredients in a bowl and mix well together. Pour the marinade over the pork and toss the meat in it until well coated. Cover the dish and leave to marinate in the refrigerator for 8 hours or overnight, stirring the pork 2–3 times.

You can use wooden or metal skewers to cook the brochettes and for this recipe you will need 12 x 15-cm/6-inch skewers. If you are using wooden ones, soak them in cold water for about 30 minutes prior to using. This helps to stop them burning and the food sticking to them during cooking. Metal skewers simply need to be greased, and flat ones should be used in preference to round ones to prevent the food on them falling off.

Preheat the grill to medium-high. Thread about 3 marinated pork pieces, leaving a little space between each piece, on to each prepared skewer. Cook the brochettes for 10–15 minutes or until tender and lightly charred, turning several times and basting with the remaining marinade during cooking. Serve the pork brochettes piping hot, garnished with parsley.

makes 12

3 slices Parma ham

3 eggs

1 poached chicken breast, shredded

12 baby gem lettuce leaves

6 anchovies cut in half lengthways

12 Parmesan shavings

cracked black pepper

for the dressing

1 tbsp mayonnaise

1 tbsp water

1 tsp white wine vinegar

miniature caesar salad

Preheat the grill to medium-high, and line the grill rack with foil.

Place the Parma ham on the grill rack, directly beneath the heat source and grill until crispy. This will not take long.

To cook the eggs, put them in a saucepan, cover with cold water and slowly bring to the boil. Immediately reduce the heat to very low, cover and simmer gently for 10 minutes. As soon as the eggs are cooked, drain them and put under cold running water until they are cold. By doing this quickly, you will prevent a black ring from forming around the egg yolk. Gently tap the eggs to crack the eggshells and leave them until cold. When cold, crack the shells all over and remove and then roughly chop the eggs.

To make the dressing, mix together the mayonnaise, water and vinegar.

To assemble, place a small amount of the chicken on each lettuce leaf and top with the dressing. Then add the egg, anchovies and Parmesan and sprinkle with black pepper. Break the Parma ham into 12 neat pieces, place on the very top of your canapés and serve.

serves 6

2 fresh tuna steaks, weighing about 250 g/9 oz in total and about 2.5 cm/1 inch thick

5 tbsp of extra virgin olive oil

3 tbsp red wine vinegar

4 sprigs of fresh thyme, plus extra to garnish

1 bay leaf

2 tbsp plain flour

1 onion, finely chopped

2 garlic cloves, finely chopped

85 g/3 oz pimiento-stuffed green olives, halved

salt and pepper

tuna with pimiento-stuffed olives

Don't get caught out with this recipe – the tuna steaks need to be marinated, so remember to start preparing the dish the day before you are going to serve it. Remove the skin from the tuna steaks, then cut the steaks in half along the grain of the fish. Cut each half into 1-cm/½-inch thick slices against the grain.

Put 3 tablespoons of the olive oil and the vinegar in a large, shallow, non-metallic dish. Strip the leaves from the sprigs of thyme and add these to the dish with the bay leaf and salt and pepper to taste. Add the prepared strips of tuna, cover the dish and leave to marinate in the refrigerator for 8 hours or overnight.

The next day, put the flour in a polythene bag. Remove the tuna strips from the marinade, reserving the marinade for later, add them to the bag of flour and toss well until they are lightly coated.

Heat the remaining olive oil in a large, heavy-based frying pan. Add the onion and garlic and gently fry for 5–10 minutes, or until softened and golden brown. Add the tuna strips to the pan and fry for 2–5 minutes, turning several times, until the fish becomes opaque. Add the reserved marinade and olives to the pan and cook for a further 1–2 minutes, stirring, until the fish is tender and the sauce has thickened.

Serve the tuna and olives piping hot, garnished with thyme sprigs.

Classic Bites

serves 4

125 ml/4 fl oz extra virgin olive oil

1 small oval-shaped loaf of white bread (ciabatta or bloomer), cut into 1-cm/ $1/2$-inch slices

4 tomatoes, deseeded and diced

6 fresh basil leaves, torn, plus extra for garnish

8 black olives, stoned and chopped

1 large garlic clove, peeled and halved

salt and pepper

olive & tomato bruschetta

Pour half the oil into a shallow dish and place the bread in it. Leave for 1–2 minutes, then turn and leave for a further 2 minutes. The bread should be thoroughly saturated in the oil.

Meanwhile, put the tomatoes into a mixing bowl. Tear the basil leaves into pieces and sprinkle over the tomatoes. Season to taste with salt and pepper and add the olives. Pour over the remaining oil and leave to marinate while you toast the bruschetta.

Preheat the grill to medium. Place the bread on the grill rack and cook for 2 minutes on each side, or until golden and crisp.

Remove the bread from the grill and arrange on a plate.

Rub the cut edge of the garlic halves over the surface of the bruschetta, then top each slice with a spoonful of the tomato mixture. Serve immediately, garnished with basil leaves.

makes 16

1 potato, cut into chunks

pinch of salt

4 spring onions, chopped

1 garlic clove, chopped

1 tbsp chopped fresh thyme

1 tbsp chopped fresh basil

1 tbsp chopped fresh coriander

225 g/8 oz white crabmeat, drained if canned and thawed if frozen

1/2 tsp Dijon mustard

1/2 fresh green chilli, deseeded and finely chopped

1 egg, lightly beaten

plain flour, for dusting

sunflower oil, for frying

pepper

lime wedges, to garnish

dip or salsa of choice, to serve

crab cakes

Place the potato in a small saucepan and add water to cover. Add the salt. Bring to the boil, then reduce the heat, cover and simmer for 10–15 minutes, or until softened. Drain well, turn into a large bowl and mash with a potato masher or fork until smooth.

Meanwhile, place the spring onions, garlic, thyme, basil and coriander in a mortar and pound with a pestle until smooth. Add the herb paste to the mashed potato with the crabmeat, mustard, chilli, egg and pepper to taste. Mix well, cover with clingfilm and chill in the refrigerator for 30 minutes.

Sprinkle flour onto a shallow plate. Shape spoonfuls of the crabmeat mixture into small balls with your hands, then flatten slightly and dust with flour, shaking off any excess. Heat the oil in a frying pan over a high heat, add the crab cakes, in batches, and cook for 2–3 minutes on each side until golden. Remove from the pan and drain on kitchen paper. Set aside to cool to room temperature.

Arrange the crab cakes on a serving dish and garnish with lime wedges. Serve with a bowl of dip or salsa.

meatballs in almond sauce

serves 6–8

55 g/2 oz white or brown bread, crusts removed

3 tbsp water

450 g/1 lb fresh lean pork mince

1 large onion, finely chopped

1 garlic clove, crushed

2 tbsp chopped fresh flat-leaf parsley, plus extra to garnish

1 egg, beaten

freshly grated nutmeg

flour, for coating

2 tbsp extra virgin olive oil

squeeze of lemon juice

salt and pepper

crusty bread, to serve

for the almond sauce

2 tbsp olive oil

25 g/1 oz white or brown bread

115 g/4 oz blanched almonds

2 garlic cloves, finely chopped

150 ml/5 fl oz dry white wine

425 ml/15 fl oz vegetable stock

salt and pepper

To prepare the meatballs, put the bread in a bowl, add the water and soak for 5 minutes. With your hands, squeeze out the water and return the bread to the dried bowl. Add the pork, onion, garlic, parsley and egg, then season with nutmeg, and salt and pepper. Knead the ingredients together to form a smooth mixture.

Spread some flour on a plate. With floured hands, shape the meat mixture into about 30 equal-sized balls, then roll each meatball again in flour until coated.

Heat the olive oil in a large, heavy-based frying pan, add the meatballs, in batches so that they do not overcrowd the pan, and fry for 4–5 minutes, or until browned on all sides. Using a slotted spoon, remove the meatballs from the pan and set aside.

To make the almond sauce, heat the oil in the same frying pan in which the meatballs were cooked. Break the bread into pieces, add to the pan with the almonds and cook, stirring frequently, until the bread and almonds are golden. Add the garlic and cook for 30 seconds, then pour in the wine and boil for 1–2 minutes. Season to taste with salt and pepper and let cool.

Transfer the almond mixture to a food processor. Pour in the vegetable stock and blend the mixture until smooth. Return the sauce to the frying pan.

Carefully add the cooked meatballs to the sauce and simmer for 25 minutes, or until the meatballs are tender. Taste and season with salt and pepper if necessary. Transfer the cooked meatballs and sauce to a warmed serving dish, add a squeeze of lemon and garnish with chopped parsley. Serve hot accompanied by slices of crusty bread.

serves 12

350 g/12 oz long-grain rice

450 g/1 lb vine leaves, rinsed if preserved in brine

2 onions, finely chopped

1 bunch spring onions, finely chopped

1 bunch fresh parsley, finely chopped

25 g/1 oz fresh mint, finely chopped

1 tbsp fennel seeds

1 tsp crushed dried chillies

finely grated rind of 2 lemons

225 ml/8 fl oz extra virgin olive oil

600 ml/1 pint boiling water

salt

stuffed vine leaves

Bring a large saucepan of lightly salted water to the boil. Add the rice and return to the boil. Reduce the heat and simmer for 15 minutes, or until tender.

Meanwhile, if using preserved vine leaves, place them in a heatproof bowl and pour over boiling water to cover. Set aside to soak for 10 minutes. If using fresh vine leaves, bring a saucepan of water to the boil, add the vine leaves, then reduce the heat and simmer for 10 minutes.

Drain the rice and, while still hot, mix with the onions, spring onions, parsley, mint, fennel seeds, chillies, lemon rind and 3 tablespoons of the oil in a large bowl. Season to taste with salt.

Drain the vine leaves well. Spread out 1 leaf, vein side up, on a work surface. Place a generous teaspoonful of the rice mixture on the leaf near the stalk. Fold the stalk end over the filling, fold in the sides and roll up the leaf. Repeat until all the filling has been used. There may be some vine leaves left over – you can use them to line a serving platter, if wished.

Place the parcels in a large, heavy-based saucepan in a single layer (you may need to use 2 saucepans). Spoon over the remaining oil, then add the boiling water. Cover the parcels with an inverted heatproof plate to keep them below the surface of the water, cover the saucepan and simmer for 1 hour.

Allow the parcels to cool to room temperature in the saucepan, then transfer to a serving platter with a slotted spoon.

makes 40

55 g/2 oz canned anchovy fillets in olive oil, drained and roughly chopped

55 g/2 oz black olives, stoned and roughly chopped

115 g/4 oz Manchego or Cheddar cheese, finely grated

115 g/4 oz plain flour, plus extra for dusting

115 g/4 oz unsalted butter, diced

1/2 tsp cayenne pepper, plus extra for dusting

anchovy, olive & cheese triangles

Place the anchovies, olives, cheese, flour, butter and cayenne pepper in a food processor and pulse until a dough forms. Turn out and shape into a ball. Wrap in foil and chill in the refrigerator for 30 minutes.

Preheat the oven to 200°C/400°F/Gas Mark 6. Unwrap the dough, knead on a lightly floured work surface and roll out thinly. Using a sharp knife, cut it into strips about 5-cm/2-inches wide. Cut diagonally across each strip, turning the knife in alternate directions, to make triangles.

Arrange the triangles on 2 baking sheets and dust lightly with cayenne pepper. Bake in the preheated oven for 10 minutes, or until golden brown. Transfer to wire racks to cool completely.

makes 16

8 large eggs

2 whole pimientos (sweet red peppers) from a jar or can

8 green olives

5 tbsp mayonnaise

8 drops Tabasco sauce

large pinch cayenne pepper

salt and pepper

sprigs of fresh dill, to garnish

devilled eggs

To cook the eggs, put them in a saucepan, cover with cold water and slowly bring to the boil. Immediately reduce the heat to very low, cover and simmer gently for 10 minutes. As soon as the eggs are cooked, drain them and put under cold running water until they are cold. By doing this quickly, you will prevent a black ring from forming around the egg yolk. Gently tap the eggs to crack the eggshells and leave them until cold. When cold, crack the shells all over and remove them.

Using a stainless steel knife, halve the eggs lengthways, then carefully remove the yolks. Put the yolks in a nylon sieve, set over a bowl, and rub through, then mash them with a wooden spoon or fork. If necessary, rinse the egg whites under cold water and dry very carefully.

Put the pimientos on kitchen paper to dry well, then chop them finely, reserving a few strips. Finely chop the olives. If you are going to pipe the filling into the eggs, you need to chop both these ingredients very finely so that they will go through a 1-cm/½-inch nozzle. Add the chopped pimientos and most of the chopped olives to the mashed egg yolks, reserving 16 larger pieces for garnish. Add the mayonnaise, mix well together, then add the Tabasco sauce, cayenne pepper and salt and pepper to taste.

Using a piping bag with a 1 cm/½ inch nozzle or a teaspoon, pipe or spoon the filling into each egg half. Arrange the eggs on a serving plate and add a small strip of the reserved pimientos and a piece of olive to the top of each stuffed egg. Garnish with dill sprigs and serve.

serves 8

450 g/1 lb can or jar unstoned large green olives, drained

4 garlic cloves, peeled

2 tsp coriander seeds

1 small lemon

4 sprigs of fresh thyme

4 feathery stalks of fennel

2 small fresh red chillies (optional)

extra virgin olive oil, to cover

pepper

cracked marinated olives

To allow the flavours of the marinade to penetrate the olives, place on a chopping board and, using a rolling pin, bash them lightly so that they crack slightly. Alternatively, use a sharp knife to cut a lengthways slit in each olive as far as the stone. Using the flat side of a broad knife, lightly crush each garlic clove. Using a pestle and mortar, crack the coriander seeds. Cut the lemon, with its rind, into small chunks.

Put the olives, garlic, coriander seeds, lemon chunks, thyme sprigs, fennel and chillies, if using, in a large bowl and toss together. Season with pepper to taste, but you should not need to add salt as conserved olives are usually salty enough. Pack the ingredients tightly into a glass jar with a lid. Pour in enough olive oil to cover the olives, then seal the jar tightly.

Leave the olives at room temperature for 24 hours, then marinate in the refrigerator for at least 1 week but preferably 2 weeks before serving. From time to time, gently give the jar a shake to re-mix the ingredients. Return the olives to room temperature and remove from the oil to serve. Provide cocktail sticks for spearing the olives.

serves 6

450 g/1 lb button mushrooms

5 tbsp olive oil

2 garlic cloves, finely chopped

squeeze of lemon juice

4 tbsp chopped fresh flat-leaf
parsley

salt and pepper

crusty bread, to serve

sautéed garlic
mushrooms

Wipe or brush clean the mushrooms, then trim off the stalks close to the caps. Cut any large mushrooms in half or into quarters. Heat the olive oil in a large, heavy-based frying pan, add the garlic and fry for 30 seconds–1 minute, or until lightly browned. Add the mushrooms and sauté over a high heat, stirring most of the time, until the mushrooms have absorbed all the oil in the pan.

Reduce the heat to low. When the juices have come out of the mushrooms, increase the heat again and sauté for 4–5 minutes, stirring most of the time, until the juices have almost evaporated. Add a squeeze of lemon juice and season to taste with salt and pepper. Stir in the parsley and cook for a further minute.

Transfer the sautéed mushrooms to a warmed serving dish and serve piping hot or warm. Accompany with chunks or slices of crusty bread for mopping up the garlic cooking juices.

serves 6–8

450 g/1 lb baby new potatoes

1 tbsp chopped fresh flat-leaf parsley

salt

for the aïoli

see page 87 for ingredients and method

baby potatoes with aïoli

To make the aïoli, follow the method on page 87. However, for this recipe the aïoli should be a little thinner so that it coats the potatoes. To ensure this, quickly blend in 1 tablespoon of water so that it forms the consistency of a sauce.

To prepare the potatoes, cut them in half or quarters to make bite-size pieces. If they are very small, you can leave them whole. Put the potatoes in a large saucepan of cold, salted water and bring to the boil. Reduce the heat and simmer for 7 minutes, or until just tender. Drain well, then turn out into a large bowl.

While the potatoes are still warm, pour over the aïoli sauce and gently toss the potatoes in it. Adding the sauce to the potatoes while they are still warm will help them to absorb the garlic flavour. Leave for about 20 minutes to allow the potatoes to marinate in the sauce.

Transfer the potatoes with aïoli to a warmed serving dish, sprinkle over the parsley and salt to taste and serve warm. Alternatively, the dish can be prepared ahead and stored in the refrigerator, but return it to room temperature before serving.

serves 6

4 limes

12 raw king prawns, in their shells

3 tbsp extra virgin olive oil

2 garlic cloves, finely chopped

splash of dry sherry

4 tbsp chopped fresh flat-leaf parsley

salt and pepper

lime-drizzled prawns

Grate the rind and squeeze out the juice from 2 of the limes. Cut the remaining 2 limes into wedges and reserve for later.

To prepare the prawns, remove the legs, leaving the shells and tails intact. Using a sharp knife, make a shallow slit along the back of each prawn, then pull out the dark vein and discard. Rinse the prawns under cold water and dry well on kitchen paper.

Heat the olive oil in a large, heavy-based frying pan, then add the garlic and fry for 30 seconds. Add the prawns and fry for 5 minutes, stirring from time to time, or until they turn pink and begin to curl. Mix in the lime rind, juice and a splash of sherry to moisten, then stir well together.

Transfer the cooked prawns to a serving dish, season to taste with salt and pepper and sprinkle over the parsley. Serve piping hot, accompanied by the reserved lime wedges for squeezing over the prawns.

Dips & Spreads

serves 6

225 g/8 oz cooked or drained
canned chickpeas

150 ml/5 fl oz tahini, well
stirred

150 ml/5 fl oz olive oil, plus
extra to serve

2 garlic cloves, coarsely
chopped

6 tbsp lemon juice

1 tbsp chopped fresh mint

salt and pepper

1 tsp paprika

hummus

Put the chickpeas, tahini, olive oil and 150 ml/5 fl oz water into the blender and process briefly. Add the garlic, lemon juice and mint and process until smooth.

Check the consistency of the hummus and, if it is too thick, add 1 tablespoon water and process again. Continue adding water, 1 tablespoon at a time, until the right consistency is achieved. Hummus should have a thick, coating consistency. Season with salt and pepper.

Spoon the hummus into a serving dish. Make a shallow hollow in the top and drizzle with 2–3 tablespoons olive oil. Cover with clingfilm and chill until required. To serve, dust lightly with paprika.

serves 6

2 slices white bread, crusts
removed

5 tbsp milk

225 g/8 oz smoked cod's roe

2 garlic cloves, coarsely
chopped

150 ml/5 fl oz olive oil

2 tbsp lemon juice

2 tbsp natural Greek-style
yogurt

pepper

black olives, to garnish

taramasalata

Tear the bread into pieces and place in a shallow bowl. Add
the milk and set aside to soak. Meanwhile, using a sharp knife,
scrape the cod's roe away from the outer skin.

Tip the bread and milk into a blender and process until smooth.
Add the cod's roe and garlic and process again. With the motor
running, gradually pour in the olive oil through the feeder tube.
Process until smooth and the consistency of mayonnaise.

Add the lemon juice and yogurt and season with pepper. Process
very briefly to mix, then scrape into a bowl. Cover with clingfilm
and chill in the refrigerator until required. Garnish with black
olives to serve.

serves 6

juice of 1 lime

3 avocados

2 garlic cloves, chopped

3 spring onions, chopped

2 fresh green chillies,
deseeded and chopped

2 tbsp olive oil

1 tbsp soured cream

salt

cayenne pepper, to garnish

tortilla chips, to serve

guacamole

Put the lime juice into the blender. Halve the avocados and remove the stones. Scoop out the avocado flesh with a spoon straight into the blender.

Add the garlic, spring onions, chillies, olive oil and soured cream and season with salt. Process until smooth. Taste and adjust the seasoning with more salt or lime juice.

Spoon the guacamole into a serving dish. Dust lightly with cayenne pepper and serve with tortilla chips.

serves 6–8

2 large aubergines

2 red peppers

4 tbsp olive oil

2 garlic cloves, roughly chopped

grated rind and juice of 1/2 lemon

1 tbsp chopped fresh coriander

1/2–1 tsp paprika

salt and pepper

bread or toast, to serve

aubergine & pepper dip

Preheat the oven to 190°C/375°F/Gas Mark 5. Prick the skins of the aubergines and peppers all over with a fork and brush with about 1 tablespoon of the olive oil. Put on a baking tray and bake in the oven for 45 minutes, or until the skins are beginning to turn black, the flesh of the aubergine is very soft and the peppers are deflated.

When the vegetables are cooked, put them in a bowl and immediately cover tightly with a clean, damp tea towel. Alternatively, you can put the vegetables in a polythene bag. Leave them for about 15 minutes until they are cool enough to handle.

When the vegetables have cooled, cut the aubergines in half lengthways, carefully scoop out the flesh and discard the skin. Cut the aubergine flesh into large chunks. Remove and discard the stem, core and seeds from the peppers and cut the flesh into large pieces.

Heat the remaining olive oil in a large, heavy-based frying pan, add the aubergine flesh and pepper pieces and fry for 5 minutes. Add the garlic and fry for a further 30 seconds.

Turn all the contents of the frying pan on to kitchen paper to drain, then transfer to the bowl of a food processor. Add the lemon rind and juice, the chopped coriander, the paprika, and salt and pepper according to taste, and blend until a speckled purée is formed.

Turn the dip into a serving bowl accompanied with thick slices of bread or toast.

serves 6

225 g/8 oz chicken livers

140 g/5 oz butter

2 garlic cloves, coarsely chopped

2 tsp chopped fresh sage leaves

2 tbsp Marsala wine

150 ml/5 fl oz double cream

salt and pepper

55 g/2 oz butter and 4–6 fresh sage leaves, to garnish

chicken liver pâté

Trim the chicken livers and chop coarsely. Melt 55 g/2 oz of the butter in a heavy-based frying pan. Add the chicken livers and cook over a medium heat for 5–8 minutes until browned all over but still pink inside. Remove the pan from the heat.

Transfer the chicken livers, in small batches, to the blender and process. Return all the livers to the blender and add the garlic, sage leaves and remaining butter. Season with salt and pepper.

Pour the Marsala into the frying pan and stir with a wooden spoon, scraping up any sediment, then add the mixture to the blender. Process until the pâté is smooth and thoroughly mixed. Add the cream and process again to mix. Spoon the pâté into individual pots and leave to cool completely.

Melt the butter for the garnish in a small saucepan over a low heat. Remove the pan from the heat and pour the melted butter over the surface of the cooled pâté. Arrange the sage leaves on top. Leave to cool, then cover with clingfilm and chill for at least 1 hour.

serves 4

3 large garlic cloves, finely chopped

2 egg yolks

225 ml/8 fl oz extra virgin olive oil

1 tbsp lemon juice

1 tbsp lime juice

1 tbsp Dijon mustard

1 tbsp chopped fresh tarragon

salt and pepper

aïoli

Ensure that all the ingredients are at room temperature. Place the garlic and egg yolks in a food processor and process until well blended. With the motor running, pour in the oil teaspoon by teaspoon through the feeder tube until the mixture starts to thicken, then pour in the remaining oil in a thin stream until a thick mayonnaise forms.

Add the lemon and lime juices, mustard and tarragon and season to taste with salt and pepper. Blend until smooth, then transfer to a non-metallic bowl.

Cover with clingfilm and refrigerate until required.

serves 4–6

200 g/7oz Greek feta cheese, crumbled

55 g/2 oz Greek yogurt

2tbsp extra virgin olive oil

zest and juice of one small lemon

small bunch of fresh mint, chopped

small bunch of fresh flat-leaf parsley, chopped

1/2 red chilli, seeded and chopped

pepper to taste

warmed pittas and some olives, to serve

herbed feta spread

Place the crumbled feta, yogurt and olive oil in a food processor and blend for 30 seconds until combined.

Scrape the mixture into a bowl and then add the lemon zest and juice, mint, parsley and chilli. Season to taste with pepper and mix well.

Leave in the refrigerator to chill for at least half an hour before serving.

Serve with the warmed pittas and the olives.

serves 4

100 g/3¹/₂ oz canned anchovy fillets

350 g/12 oz black olives, stoned and coarsely chopped

2 garlic cloves, coarsely chopped

2 tbsp capers, drained and rinsed

1 tbsp Dijon mustard

3 tbsp extra virgin olive oil

2 tbsp lemon juice

tapenade

Drain the anchovies, reserving the oil from the can. Coarsely chop the fish and place in the blender. Add the reserved oil and all the remaining ingredients. Process to a smooth purée. Stop and scrape down the sides if necessary.

Transfer the tapenade to a dish, cover with clingfilm and chill in the refrigerator until required. If you are not planning to use the tapenade until the following day (or even the one after), cover the surface with a layer of olive oil to prevent it from drying out.

serves 6

2 red peppers, halved and
deseeded

2 garlic cloves

1 tbsp extra virgin olive oil

1 tbsp lemon juice

25 g/1 oz fresh white
breadcrumbs

salt and pepper

red pepper dip

Place the pepper halves and garlic in a saucepan and add just
enough water to cover. Bring to the boil, then lower the heat,
cover and simmer gently for 10–15 minutes until softened and
tender. Drain and set aside to cool.

Coarsely chop the pepper halves and garlic and place in the
blender with the olive oil and lemon juice. Process to a smooth
purée.

Add the breadcrumbs and process briefly until just combined.
Season to taste with salt and pepper. Transfer to a serving bowl,
cover with clingfilm and chill in the refrigerator until required.

serves 6–8

250 g/9 oz whole beetroot

100 ml/3¹/₂ oz extra virgin olive oil

115 g/4 oz roasted hazelnuts

2 cloves garlic, peeled

115 g/4 oz fresh Parmesan cheese, freshly grated

salt and pepper

selection of crudités or bruschetta, to serve

beetroot & hazelnut pesto

Preheat the oven to 180°C/ 350°F/Gas Mark 5.

Sprinkle the beetroot with a little salt and pepper then drizzle with a small amount of the olive oil. Wrap the beetroot in foil and place in the oven. Cook for 1 hour. To test to see if the beetroot is cooked, poke with a small knife; the blade should go in with ease.

Remove the cooked beetroot from the oven and leave to cool. Once cool, peel away the skin and discard.

Place the hazelnuts and garlic in a food processor and process for 30 seconds.

Add the beetroot, salt and pepper and process again adding the olive oil a little at a time, through the feeder tube, until combined.

Pour the pesto into a bowl and mix in the Parmesan cheese.

Serve with crudités or spread on bruschetta.